# ROBOTS

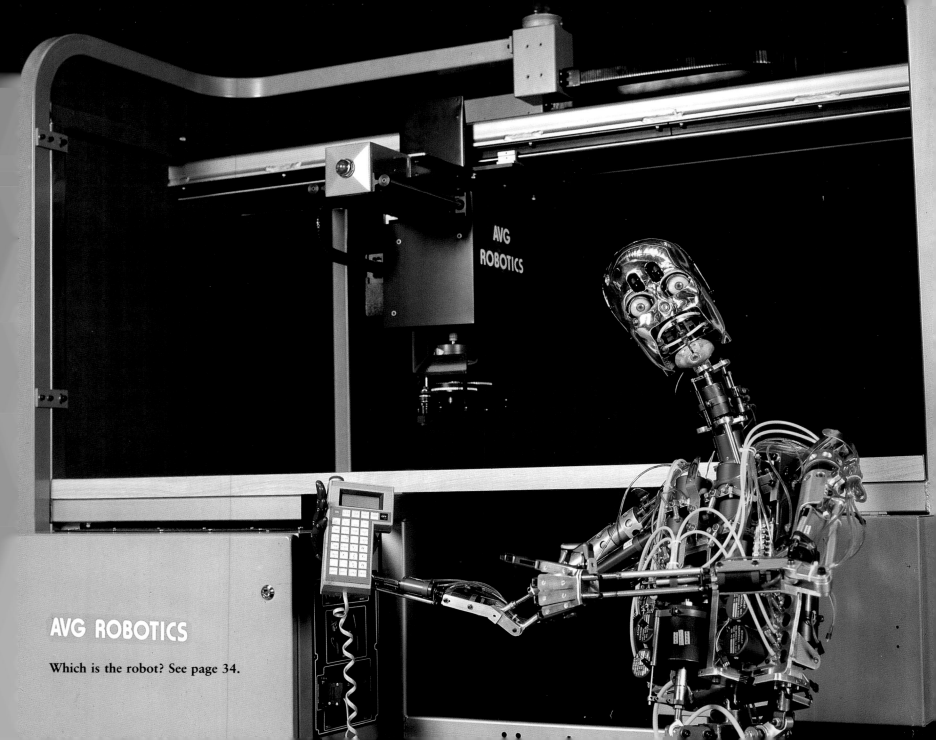

# AVG ROBOTICS

Which is the robot? See page 34.

# ROBOTS
## YOUR HIGH-TECH WORLD

*by Gloria Skurzynski*

BRADBURY PRESS / NEW YORK

*For Daniel Edward Ferguson and Katherine Alane Ferguson,*
*who will live in a world like this*

Bradbury Press
An Affiliate of Macmillan, Inc.
866 Third Avenue, New York, NY 10022
Collier Macmillan Canada, Inc.

The text of this book is set in 13 point Sabon.
Book design by Christy Hale
Bands of color on the cover and interior created by David Lui

Printed and bound in Hong Kong
First American Edition
10 9 8 7 6 5 4 3 2 1

Library of Congress Cataloging-in-Publication Data
Skurzynski, Gloria.   Robots : your high-tech world / by
Gloria Skurzynski.—1st ed.   p.   cm.
Summary: An introduction to robots and robotics, focusing on such topics
as the effect of computer advances on the development of robots in the
medical, scientific, industrial, and entertainment fields, and comparisons of
human and robotic abilities.
ISBN 0-02-782917-0
1. Robots—Juvenile literature.  [1. Robots.  2. Robotics.]  I. Title.
TJ211.2.S58     1990   629.8'92—dc20   89-70805   CIP   AC

# CONTENTS

Only rarely do today's robotic workers
look this human.

From the time of the first machines, people have dreamed about inventing imitation humans. Made of metal, wire, or wood, of springs, tubes, and cables, these mechanical creatures would be ours to command. They would work for us, protect us, and help us get ahead in the world. If we wanted companionship, they could give us that, too.

Mechanical creatures have existed for at least five hundred years, and some of them were made to look quite human. Yet they were not much more than toys. The cleverest ones could walk, talk, play musical instruments, or even write with a quill pen using real ink. They ran on springs, pegs, and cogs like the inner workings of windup clocks or music boxes. Far too expensive for ordinary people to own, these artful toys amused only royalty.

In 1921, a Czechoslovakian author named Karel Čapek wrote a play titled *R.U.R.* In it, humanlike creatures were manufactured by the millions on a remote island. They had only one

*Anyone who has looked into human anatomy will have seen at once that man is too complicated, and that a good engineer could make him more simply.*

From *R.U.R.*

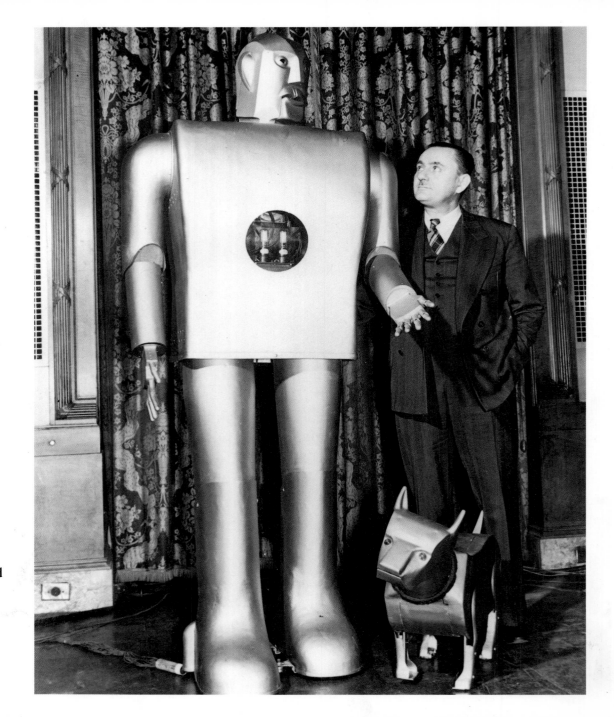

In 1939, J. M. Barnett, who invented Elektro and Sparko, declared that robots could never take the place of humans.

purpose: to work. Čapek named these fictional creatures *robots*, which is the Czech word for "workers." *R.U.R.* stood for Rossum's Universal Robots.

Robot. A strong, no-nonsense word, it's the perfect term for a servant who would never question a master's orders. The word quickly found its way into languages all over the world. Though it was an exciting idea, no one knew how to make artificial humans who could perform useful work. The technology just didn't exist.

Robots remained curiosities: At the New York World's Fair in 1939, a lumbering mechanical man named Elektro became one of the fair's most popular exhibits. Elektro had a little mechanical dog named Sparko that could walk and sit and bark on command. Westinghouse Electric & Manufacturing Company had built them both.

Inside Elektro, motors and switches moved his lips, arms, and hands as long as his cord was plugged into a socket. Photocells activated a turntable with a phonograph record that let Elektro speak seventy-seven different words. He could count to ten on his fingers, speaking the numbers out loud. He could move backward and forward. Yet Elektro and Sparko performed no really useful work except to demonstrate the wonders of electricity. Even their creator, J. M. Barnett, declared, "No engineer would ever be so ridiculous as to imagine that any robot could ever take the place of man." That was in 1939.

Today, robots still entertain people the way Electro and Sparko did, but they look a lot more realistic. Dinamation International,

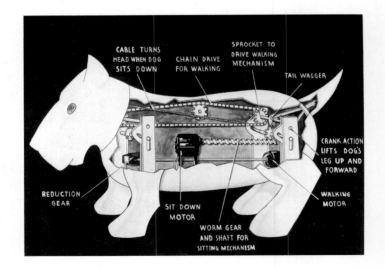

Electric current activated the motors that even let Sparko wag his tail.

Valves, pistons, rods, and compressed air make the tyrannosaur move realistically.

of San Juan Capistrano, California, has created a herd of massive robot dinosaurs. They appear in exhibits across the United States, where they growl, roar, toss their reptilian heads, twitch their tails, and lurch forward so ferociously that small children clutch their parents in fright. Since Dinamation creatures weigh about as much as their ancient, live ancestors did, it takes a lot of muscle to move them.

It may seem strange to use a biological term like *muscle* to describe a machine—and all robots are machines. Most robotic parts are called by anatomical names: arms, legs, hands, fingers, tendons, nerves, brains, and muscle. Muscle is just a way of saying "strength."

Pneumatic power—compressed air—provides the muscle for Dinamation dinosaurs. Although we live in an ocean of air, we pay little attention to it because we move through it without feeling any resistance. *Compressed air* is air that's been squeezed tightly into a small space. It can be released to blast through a hose, pushing a piston that moves a rod inside an imitation dinosaur skin—and a tyrannosaur opens huge jaws to reveal rows of meat-tearing teeth.

Robots continued to evolve with the rapid growth of technology. Twenty years after Elektro's world's fair ended, robots were no longer just novelties for entertainment. They'd begun to work in factories, where they used pneumatic power, electric power, or hydraulic power for their muscle. Hydraulic systems, which compress liquid rather than air, let industrial-robot arms lift the most weight. Robots that run on electric motors get

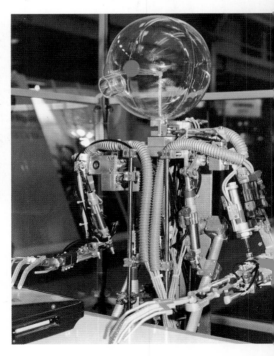

In Hanover, Germany, a demonstration robot types a program. You can see the combination of electric parts and pneumatic cylinders that drive it.

Pneumatic power is quiet enough that children can walk right up to the robot Parasaurolophus and not hear its parts move.

Factory robots don't need heads or torsos. Sometimes all they need are movable arms.

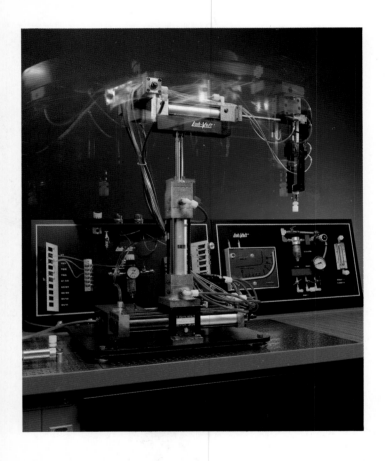

hotter and wear out faster than hydraulic ones, but electrical power has an advantage: It works more accurately because it can be divided into very small units. Since units of electricity are so much smaller than units of compressed air or hydraulic fluid, electrical power can be measured out with more exact control.

Industrial robots don't have to resemble humans or any other living creatures. For factory work, they don't require heads or torsos. What they need most are arms and hands, so that's what most of them are made of. Robot arms have elbows and wrists that let them stretch, tilt, retract, and swivel. The arms can reach up from a floor, hang down from an overhead platform, or move on rails beside a production line.

Certain robot hands, like human ones, have opposing digits. (If you can touch your fingertips with your thumb, you too have opposing digits.) In robots, these are called "grippers," and they're used to lift things that need to be moved around: "pick and place" jobs, which is a short way of saying "picking up and placing elsewhere." Robot hands can also be vacuum cups, suction cups, or magnets, which are better than grippers for lifting things like sheets of glass or thin metal.

This electrically powered robot arm can change "hands" to use, here, a gripper to pick and place.

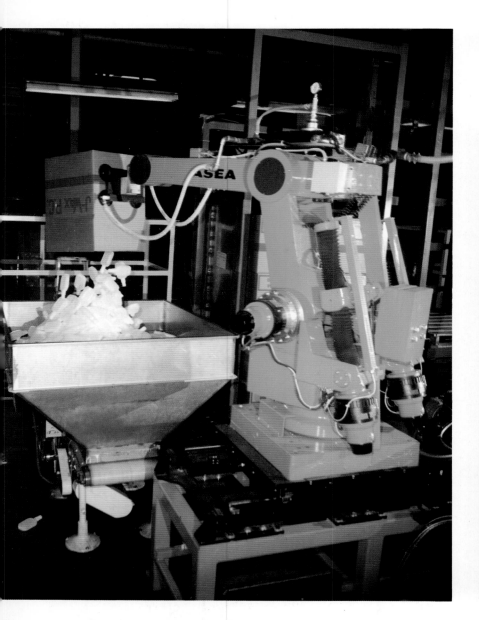

Robots don't work with tools in their hands—most often, their hands *are* the tools. Welding torches, paint sprayers, screwdrivers, drills, or ladles can be plugged into a robot wrist, then unplugged and replaced by a different tool/hand.

Factory robots are excellent at doing work humans dislike—the hot, heavy, hazardous jobs. They're especially good at boring jobs, where a human's mind might wander and cause an accident to happen. Robots don't have minds that daydream. But they do have brains.

It was the invention of electronic brains—computers—that allowed robots to become real workers at last, beginning in the 1960s. The computer revolution led to the robot revolution.

A similar robot arm can be fitted with a vacuum-cup tool/hand for bottle dumping (far left), or with an arc-welding tool/hand (left).

*End effector* is the technical name for a robot tool/hand. This end effector (right) clears away "burrs" to make a hole smooth.

This is not a robot arm because the human operator controls it directly, using levers.

Every robot working today takes its directions from a computer. That doesn't mean humans aren't involved in controlling robots. Humans instruct the computers that instruct the robots. It goes like this: humans → computers → robots. A robot will follow computer instructions endlessly until something, usually a human command, tells it to stop.

The world's first electronic digital computer, named ENIAC (Electronic Numerical Integrator and Calculator), began operating in Philadelphia, Pennsylvania, in 1946. Made with eighteen thousand glass vacuum tubes, it weighed thirty tons and spread out over fifteen hundred square feet of floor space. ENIAC was not an energy conserver: It used enough electrical power to light up a hundred lighthouses. Its vacuum tubes got extremely hot and burned out often. In spite of its drawbacks, ENIAC impressed people with its speed. It could do five thousand addition and one thousand multiplication problems in a second.

*In ten years Rossum's Universal Robots will produce so much . . . everyone will be free from worry. Man . . . will have no other aim, no other labor . . . than to perfect himself.*

From *R.U.R.*

A computer as large as ENIAC couldn't be moved; anyone who wanted to use it had to go visit it. To be more mobile and therefore more useful, computers needed to be smaller. A year after ENIAC started operating, the transistor was invented at Bell Laboratories. Transistors replaced bulky glass vacuum tubes.

Both vacuum tubes and transistors control the flow of electrons in electronic devices, but vacuum tubes are the size of whole dill pickles. Over the years, transistor designs grew smaller and smaller until today, some transistors are no bigger than bacteria. The tiniest is one micron wide, or $\frac{1}{24,000}$ of an inch.

Transistors regulate current by either blocking it or letting it pass through. On or off. Open or closed. It's exactly like a wall switch being pushed up or down to turn an electric light bulb on or off.

Whether a transistor is in the on or off position is indicated by the figures 1 or 0: 1 for *on* and 0 for *off*. These binary numbers, strings of 1s and 0s, are read by the computer as coded commands. Although the numbers sound too simple for a system that seems so complicated, the code works, and with incredible speed. On or off. Open or closed. 1 or 0. It's called machine language, and it's what computers understand.

By 1990, Bell Laboratories had created a transistor that could switch on and off electronically *140 billion* times a second. Today, the capability of computers is measured in MIPS, which stands for millions of instructions per second. (A simple instruction might be to add two binary numbers, such as 01101 and 100110. To complete that one instruction, a number of transistors need to switch on and off several times.) State-of-the-art supercomputers—the ones built with unlimited funds—operate at one hundred MIPS. That's *one hundred million* instructions per second. Compare that to ENIAC's rate.

Is there a reason for all this speed? Speed isn't so important for simple calculations, but certain problems require massive calculations. Weather forecasting is one of the major uses for supercomputers. To solve the equations and probability functions that predict weather patterns requires a great many computations. Taking even a few extra hours to forecast the course of a dangerous storm could cause loss of life. In this case, speed is crucial.

Complex collections of transistors, as many as a million of them, can be fitted on a silicon chip the size of your fingernail to form an integrated circuit. An integrated circuit, or IC, is

A printed circuit board like the one the woman is touching has wires built into it. Parts added onto the board make it a completed assembly, ready to run.

Integrated circuits, or ICs, are built up a layer at a time on a silicon wafer, in a process something like photographic printing. The tiny lines are different parts of the circuit; the squares that look like city blocks are ICs. With a laser saw, they'll be cut into identical individual chips. The entire silicon wafer (above left) is about six inches in diameter.

Custom-designed integrated circuits (above right) allow all the functions of the large board to be contained in one very small device.

found in almost every electronic product made in the past twenty-five years. ICs can vary from simple devices to the complexity of a whole computer printed on a chip. Integrated circuits are connected to each other by the traces of a printed circuit board. Certain chips on the board contain specially designed electronic parts that perform specific functions.

The smaller and faster computers became, the better they were at operating robots. Some computers operate from inside, and others from outside their robots. Since robots can now do so many different jobs, electronic parts are custom-designed for them individually.

Forty years ago, craftsmen designed, by hand, machine tools

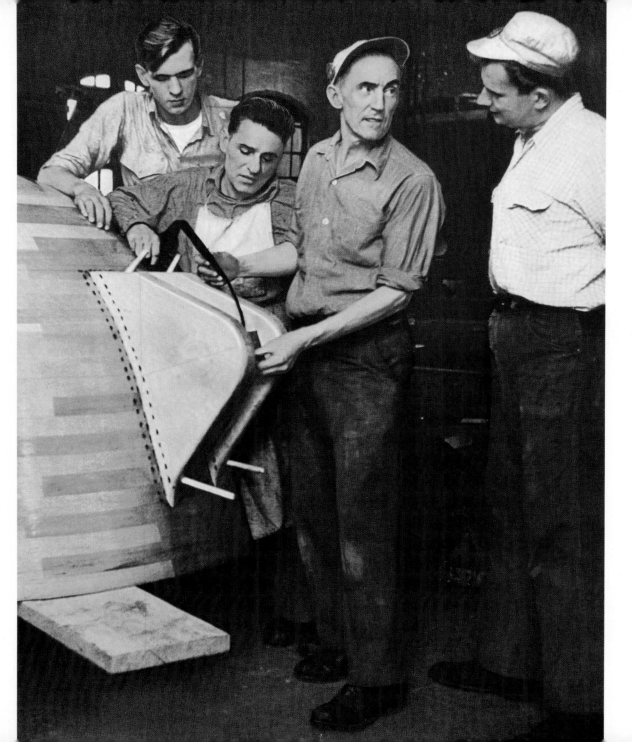

Forty years ago, craftsmen made patterns by hand for iron and steel casting.

used to build parts from plans engineers had drawn, by hand, on paper on drawing boards. Today, engineers design new products—everything from cars to aerospace components to skyscrapers—on computer screens. Interestingly, they use computers made with existing chips to create newer chips to make even better computers.

Today, products and ways to use them are designed on computer screens before they reach the factory floor.

A few decades ago, factory machines were built to perform one task and one task only. This is called *hard automation*, and it meant that production lines consisted of rows of single-purpose machines.

After the computer revolution, robots gave factories *flexible automation*, which means that each machine can be reprogrammed to do more than one job. To illustrate the difference: If you put a couple of quarters into a candy machine and push a button, the machine drops a candy bar into a slot. This is all the machine was made to do. That's hard automation. If the *same* machine could be reprogrammed to pour hot chocolate instead of vending candy bars, that would be flexible automation.

The Robot Institute of America defines *robot* this way: "a reprogrammable, multifunction manipulator, designed to move materials, parts, tools, or special devices through variable programmable motions for the performance of a variety of tasks." To be *reprogrammable*—the first requirement in the definition—a robot has to be programmable to begin with. And to be programmed, it requires a computer.

Robot production lines can be changed, in minutes, to make different products. Not with vast differences, because an automobile factory won't want to start producing panty hose, but with reasonable design changes. In Japan, the Mazak Corporation makes a variety of machine tools. Twenty-four hours a day, seven days a week, with hardly any people around, Mazak's

robots never stop making tools. To make different kinds of tools, the robots can be reprogrammed by engineers in a control room twelve miles away. If one of Mazak's smart robotic machines breaks down, it senses its own breakdown and automatically shuts itself off.

This apparent intelligence makes it hard to think of robots as just machines. Even scientists who have worked with flexible, multifunction devices for many years can start to think of them as being a bit human. When the spacecraft *Voyager 2* neared its flyby with the planet Neptune, its design manager, Charles Kohlhase, said, "We all feel affection for [the *Voyager*s]. It's sort of like we're connected to these machines. They're not human, but they are extensions of our human qualities."

Most robots do have humanlike anatomies—their arms, elbows, wrists, hands, muscle, and brains. There's a reason for this: If they're to work in place of humans, they need to fit into environments that were designed for human use. And they need body parts to carry out the work instructions human brains send them via computers. But if they aren't going to work in an environment suited for humans—underseas or in outer space or at nuclear waste sites—robots can be shaped any way at all.

These electric-driven robot arms spot-weld cars on a production line. They can be reprogrammed to do other work. That's called flexible automation.

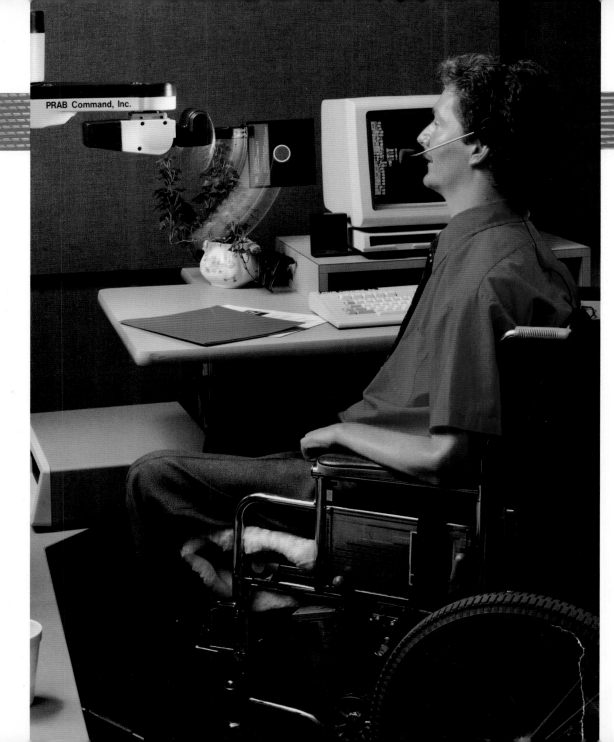

When Skip Dinger speaks to it, his robot loads a floppy disk for him.

Skip Dinger has his own robot. It does exactly what he tells it to do, and it obeys no voice but his. When Skip speaks into a small microphone next to his lips, the robot arm moves. It brings a book from a rack and places it on a stand in front of him, or loads a floppy disk into his computer disk drive. Or it can make a phone call for him to anywhere in the world. The robot is a very important part of his life, because Skip can't do any of these things for himself. He's a quadriplegic, which means he's unable to move any parts of his body from the neck down.

"On a hot day in August," Skip recalls, "some friends and I decided to go for a swim. On my third dive, cold, hard reality struck just as my head broke the surface of the water. All I heard was a loud *pop*."

The noise was his neck bone being shattered. He'd hit a picnic table submerged underwater, invisible from where he'd been diving. From then on Skip could no longer use his arms, hands, or legs. Six hundred thousand other people in the United States

Manager: *What are robots made for?*
Engineer: *For work.*
From *R.U.R.*

Senior Research Scientist Karen Engelhardt, left, believes that robots can improve the quality of life for disabled or elderly people. A robot arm plucks a flower for Mary Beth Dyke.

are quadriplegics like Skip, and each year an additional eight thousand, most of them young, become paralzyed in accidents, as Skip did, or because of disease.

The Voice Command Robotic Work Station, built by Prab Robots, Inc., allows people like Skip Dinger to work at useful jobs again. In just a few minutes, the Voice Command System can be taught to recognize the user's voice and only that voice, even if it changes somewhat (for instance, if the person has a cold).

To program the system, the user says a command aloud. That sound is broken down into acoustical signals that are translated into computer codes of 1s and 0s, which are stored in the system's computer memory. When the user says the command again, the computer searches its memory till it matches the acoustical pattern, identifying which command it is to follow. But the user has to say the commands the same way each time. Skip can't tell his robot, "Please put the floppy disk in the disk drive" if the computer has been programmed to respond to "Load the floppy disk."

At Carnegie-Mellon University in Pittsburgh, Pennsylvania, research scientist Karen G. Engelhardt creates new ways for robots to assist disabled or elderly people. She envisions a robot arm reaching down from a ceiling track for patients to lean on as they move through the halls of nursing homes. Says Engelhardt, "These 'people walkers' would be programmed to work at varying speeds, under computer control." A voice-controlled robot could lift patients, she predicts, "so that they could say

'Up,' or 'Move me down slowly.' Then [the patients] are in control."

Robots are already hard at work performing jobs that would be dangerous for human beings. They spray paints whose fumes might be explosive, or apply mists of fine metallic particles that might cause cancer if inhaled. And robots can climb to heights where people would be in jeopardy.

In Tennessee, a huge electrical-power generating plant had a problem. Kids with BB guns kept shooting out insulator caps on the high-voltage power lines. To locate the broken insulator caps, helicopter pilots had to fly so low along the wires that they sometimes crashed.

To solve this problem, Transitions Research Corporation of Danbury, Connecticut, is developing a very special robot. It can slide along the high-tension wires, climb the towers, inspect for breakage, take pictures, and report the location of the broken insulators to ground crews.

Says Gay Bogardus of TRC, "It scrunches itself up and over, and continues to grasp and release the line until it's around the tower. We call it our monkey robot, because it's the same move-ment a monkey makes to go along in the trees—one hand over the other." If people who don't know about this robot saw it zipping along power wires and skittering up towers, they might think aliens had landed in Tennessee.

Another high climber is Skywasher, made by International Robot Technologies of Marina del Rey, California. On six legs with suction-cup feet, Skywasher crawls along the outside of

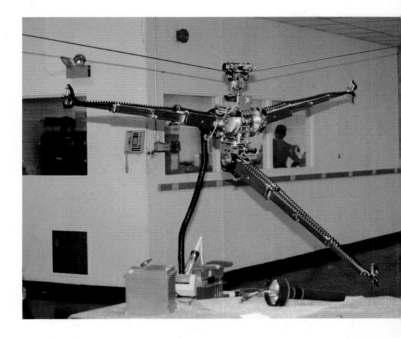

Many robots are created, as this power line inspector was, to fill a special need. Others are more experimental. Some will become widely used; others won't find a ready market. All advance the technology of robots.

Surefooted as a caterpillar, Skywasher scales walls on suction-cup feet.

tall buildings, cleaning windows as it goes. Washing fluid squirts through its hose, and three wiper blades on its underside leave glass sparkling clean.

Robots not only keep people safer, they're also helping sheep. Human sheep shearers get paid according to the number of sheep they shear each day. Naturally, this makes them work as fast as possible, and sometimes, in their hurry to snip off the fleece, they gash the sheep. To prevent infection, they'll slap a brushful of black tar on the cut, which is not very pleasant for the sheep.

Could a robot shear a living, breathing, squirming sheep safely? At the University of Western Australia, mechanical engineers went to work to invent Shear Magic, a hydraulically powered robot arm. Programmed with a map of the sheep's surface shape, Shear Magic, soon to be operational, will be able to clip a whole sheep in four minutes, with all the fleece removed in one piece.

Clothing made of wool, cotton, or man-made fibers gives little protection for people working in hazardous environments: fire fighters, for instance, or workers disposing of toxic wastes, or soldiers who might be bombarded with poisonous sprays or gases on the battlefield.

Battelle's Pacific Northwest Laboratories in Richland, Washington, designed Manny, probably the most human-looking robot ever built for work. Dressed in protective gear, Manny is placed in an eight-by-ten-foot room, where his clothes encounter toxic materials such as nerve gas or blistering agents. Manny walks, crawls, and creeps just as a real soldier would, exposing

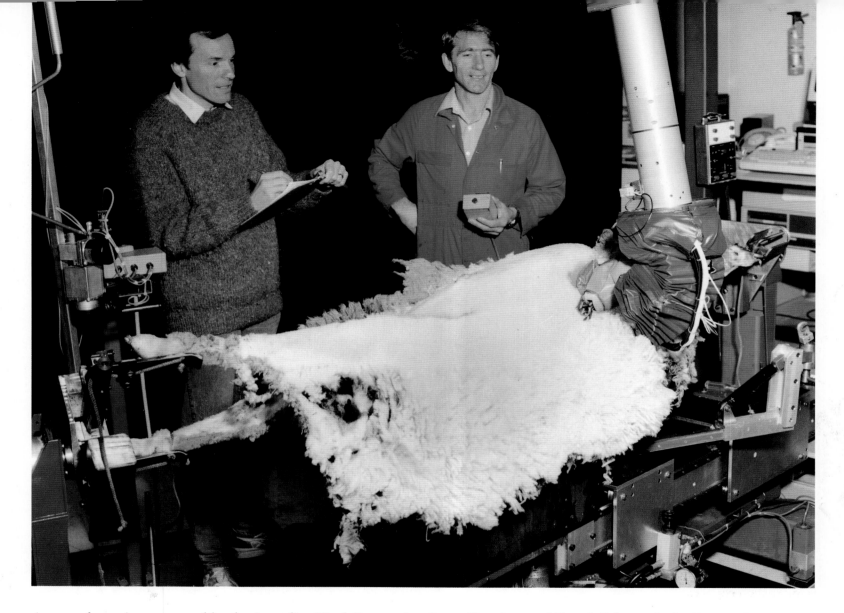

As part of a project supported by the Australian Wool Corporation, James Trevelyan and Darryl Cole watch the Shear Magic robot fleece a live sheep in Australia.

every seam of his clothing. Obviously, no real soldier could endure such danger just to test equipment, so Battelle created Manny to do the job. He's pictured on page six.

Along an aisle in a warehouse in Edison, New Jersey, a strange creature cruises on wheels at two miles per hour. It looks like a cross between Darth Vader and a brand-new trash can, but it's actually Sentry I, the security robot manufactured by Denning Mobile Robotics, Inc.

On a dark summer night in 1987, Sentry's microwave antennae sensed the presence of people on the roof. The robot flashed an electronic alarm to the human security guard at the front desk, and the guard came running. When a second guard joined the first, the intruders fled. Sentry was the first robot ever to foil an attempted burglary.

The Heath Company's robot, Hero 2000, can be bought and assembled from a kit, making it possible for you to build a robot of your very own (if you happen to have the necessary three thousand dollars). High schools buy Hero to teach students how robots are put together. Hero also helps disabled children. "It's a wonderful toy for children in a wheelchair," says the director of a rehabilitation center in Canada. "They can manipulate a very large, exciting toy that walks and talks."

Hero is a real robot, though, rather than just a moving toy. Most toys that run or fly are controlled by remote handling radio devices. You can push the buttons on a transmitter to send radio waves that maneuver the flight of a model airplane. It is not a robot, because you control it directly. But if the toy

Hero 2000 speaks nearly a thousand sentences, including the boast, "I'm the smartest robot yet."

After patrol, Sentry I returns to its charging station.

In the first-ever case of a robot stopping a real crime, the Denning security robot prevented a break-in.

plane took off, flew, and landed by itself, directed only by its own computer software, it would be a robot. Hero's computer software lets him map out space in a room and move around without bumping into furniture or people's legs. He can turn lights on and off, answer doors, and speak. All his instructions come from his computer program. That makes him a robot.

Even though today working robots outnumber entertainment robots, the entertainment robots have become so sophisticated they seem alive. If clunky Elektro impressed the crowds at the New York World's Fair in 1939, the incredibly lifelike Abraham Lincoln positively dazzled audiences at the New York World's Fair of 1964. The Lincoln robot later went to Disneyland to entertain visitors there, along with other realistic Disney robots.

The technology of entertainment robots is as complex as that of working robots. AVG, Inc., of Valencia, California, makes moving animals and monsters, aliens and humans, in a building the employees call the "fantasy factory." Yet when the Singer Company required industrial sewing equipment, AVG was able to make that too, using much of the same robotic technology. On the frontispiece of this book are two AVG robots. The entertainment robot is shown pushing a button to start up the industrial robot.

**A chorus line of entertainment robots wearing nothing but steel skeletons waits for shipment to the world's greatest amusement park.**

At Waseda University in Tokyo, Japan, a robot named Wabot-2 plays the organ. His fingers press the upper and lower keyboards, his left foot works the bass keyboard, and his right foot operates the expression pedal. He can read sheet music. He knows how to change keys to match a singer's pitch.

Wabot's a great entertainer, but he's also a highly sophisticated robot. His movements are controlled by fifty-three microprocessors. (A microprocessor isn't a complete computer; it's a central processor unit enclosed on one integrated circuit package. When it's combined with memory and input/output capabilities, a microprocessor becomes a computer on a chip— a microcomputer.) Wabot has a vision system, a speech recognition system similar to Prab's Voice Command, and a good vocabulary to talk with. It's hard to think of Wabot-2 as a mere machine, but that's exactly what he is. Every robot is a machine, but some are more intelligent than others.

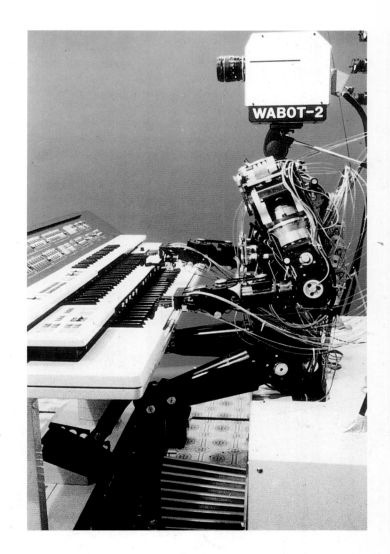

Wabot is a highly sophisticated, state-of-the-art, high-tech Japanese organ-playing robot.

Dr. Yik San Kwoh named the brain-surgery robot after his research program's benefactor.

Robots now work in every imaginable location: beneath the seas, in outer space, even inside the human brain.

In the 1960s, a young student from Hong Kong came to the United States to study electrical engineering. After Yik San Kwoh earned his Ph.D., he began to do research at the Long Beach Memorial Medical Center, in California. Interestingly, Dr. Kwoh's research was funded by a donation from another immigrant, Svend Olsen, who had come to Long Beach from Denmark forty years earlier.

The research led to a robot called Ole, named after the late Svend Olsen. Ole (pronounced OH-lee) has made medical history by performing surgery on the human brain.

Ordinarily, when a patient is suspected of having a brain tumor, the surgeon drills a nickel-sized hole in the skull. The surgeon then estimates in which direction, and how deeply, to insert the probe to remove tissue for a biopsy.

Because Ole is accurate to $\frac{1}{2,000}$ of an inch when performing

*You are not as strong as the Robots. You are not as skillful as the Robots. The Robots can do everything. You only give orders.*

From *R.U.R.*

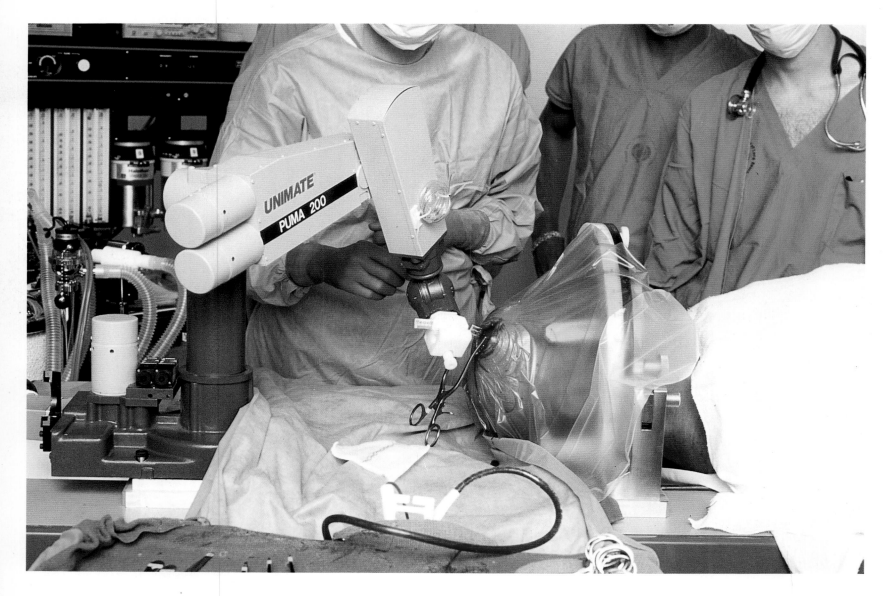

The robot called Ole can be more accurate at brain biopsies than human surgeons can.

surgery, the opening in the patient's skull can be as small as ⅛ of an inch. "Any time we reduce the size of the hole, we cut down on postoperative complications," a neurosurgeon at Long Beach Memorial Medical Center says.

Even the normal pulsing of blood in a human surgeon's fingertips can cause minute movement of the fingers. Since a robot has no pulse, there's no wavering whatever when Ole inserts the biopsy needle. And the less the brain tissue is disturbed, the better off the patient will be.

Samples of suspicious tissue must sometimes be taken from increasingly deeper points within a patient's brain. The robot is so accurate that in repeat probes, the needle can find and follow its own original path. A human surgeon's hands could never have that kind of dexterity or be so accurate.

Eye surgery demands even more precision than brain surgery. Many new microsurgery techniques require movements so infinitely small they're impossible for human hands to perform, but not for robot hands. Yet during surgery, robot movements must *always* be guided by a human surgeon.

The movements are miniaturized by *down-sizing*. If the surgeon's hand moves one inch, the robotic hand moves only one-sixteenth of an inch. If the surgeon pushes with a pound of pressure, "it lets an ounce [of pressure] come out the other end of the machine," says Dr. Steve Charles, who's developing a precision microrobot for delicate surgery on eyes, ears, hands, and brains. A microrobot is one that can make very small movements.

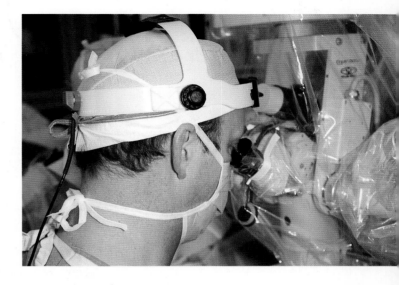

Head movements of Dr. Steve Charles cause the microscope to move. The same technology is used in fighter aircraft, where pilots have a positioning sensor, called a heads-up display, built into their helmets.

Dr. Charles, engineer Roy Williams, and their team work together at a laboratory in Memphis, Tennessee. In tests, the surgeon's hands guide robotic arms that hold miniaturized surgical tools. Dr. Charles's head movements direct an electronically positioned microscope that lets him view the operating site as he works.

The system, called telemicrorobotics (tele-micro-robotics), has not yet been tested on live patients. Dr. Charles believes that when it's perfected, operations can be performed across great distances. By remote control, and using televised satellite images

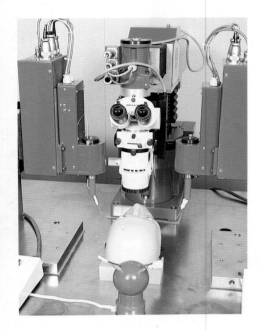

Two robot arms hold the tools for delicate eye surgery.

A satellite transmission link will let microsurgery be performed across great distances.

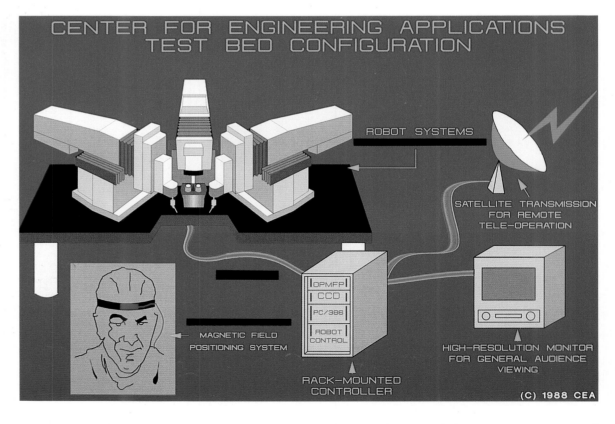

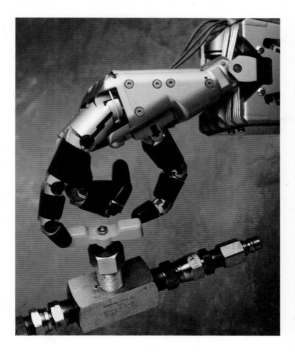

to follow the procedure, a specialist will be able to operate on a patient in a faraway, underdeveloped country where there's no up-to-date medical care. Or a surgeon on Earth could perform an operation on an astronaut in a space station.

When equipment is made to work across distances, great or small, it's called teleoperation. If a person puts a hand into a "master hand" that contains electronic controls, every motion of the human fingers can be duplicated exactly by a "slave hand." As always, a computer program links the two. *Slave* is an unpleasant word; in this case it only means that the human operator acts and the robot hand reacts with instant, matching motion. Slave hands can work with toxic or radioactive or other dangerous materials to keep human hands unharmed.

The drive system of the Utah/MIT
Dexterous Hand is both electric
and pneumatic.
The slave hand (above left) will
duplicate every movement of a master
hand (above). Electronic signals link them.

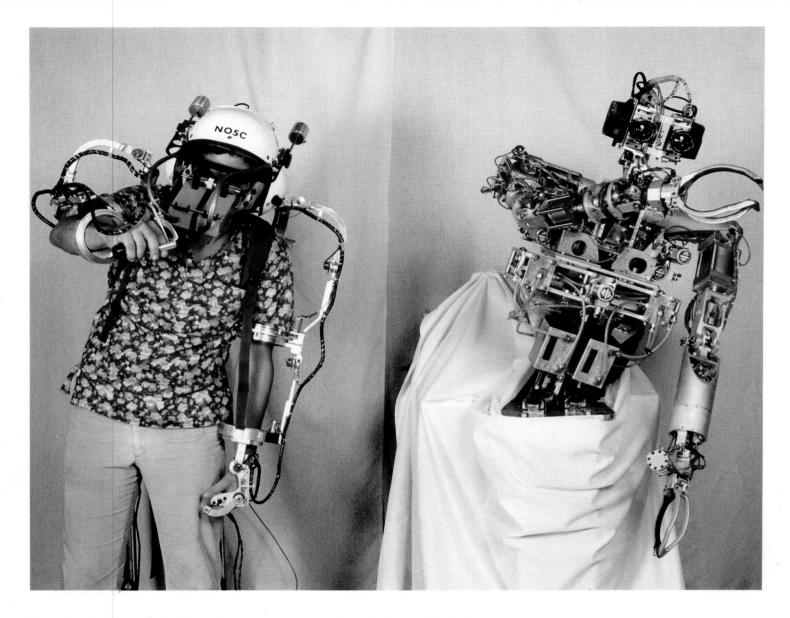

Since the teleoperator duplicates human movements, it needs humanlike body parts.

Teleoperation isn't limited to the manipulation of robot hands. It's also used to work cameras or to drive vehicles or to sample planetary soil in places where it would be dangerous or difficult for humans to go—underseas, for example.

At the Naval Ocean Systems Center in San Diego, California, a remote work system teleoperator is being developed for undersea salvage operations. Safe and dry, the master will be able to see and hear everything the slave encounters as it moves about, mimicking the master's every move. Some scientists believe that teleoperators are not true robots. They say a real robot operates without human intervention, doing only what it is programmed to do. A device controlled entirely by humans

Developed at the Naval Ocean Systems Center, this teleoperator can tie a knot.

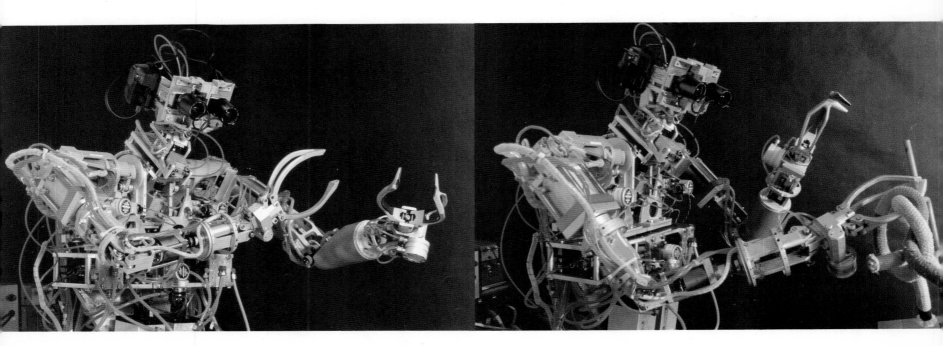

A SeaROVER is lowered over the side to do some underwater searching.

should be called a teleoperator, they believe. But most people use the term "robot."

Signals to a teleoperated robot can be sent electronically, by radio signals, or by fiber optics. A multi-conductor cable connects a human operator aboard ship to SeaROVER, a robot that starred in the movie *The Abyss*. Developed by Benthos, Inc., of North Falmouth, Massachusetts, SeaROVER can ex-

A smaller model of the SeaROVER (above) explores the ocean floor.

Shown as a thin, curved line (left), a cable carries signals between the ship and the undersea rover.

The Autonomous Land Vehicle can decide to change its programmed course.

plore the ocean floor at speeds of up to five knots. The ROV in its name stands for Remotely Operated Vehicle. With TV cameras and sonar equipment directed by the human operator topside, undersea rovers search for sunken ships, map underwater oil fields, inspect dams and pipelines, and examine marine life.

Most teleoperated robots are hybrids, responding part of the time to human control, other times operating entirely from computer programs without additional human input. Certain robots have become so independent they can even solve their own problems.

In Denver, Colorado, the Martin Marietta Corporation designed an Autonomous Land Vehicle that made certain decisions on its own. The ALV was really a robot, although it looked more like a tank. Television cameras, lasers, and radar sensors, feeding information to the ALV's computer, let it see what was ahead as it rolled along unknown terrain. If there was an obstacle in its path, the ALV could decide to take a different course from the one it was programmed to go on, letting it miss the obstacle.

That kind of independence will be very useful in rovers made to explore planets. Planetary robots have a problem other teleoperated robots don't have. Radio signals take a long time to cross the great distances between Earth, the moon, and the planets—anywhere from six to forty minutes round trip from Earth to Mars, depending on where Mars and Earth happen to be in their orbits.

If a Mars rover were completely controlled by a human on

Earth, the lag time in signal transmission would create serious problems. The camera on the moving rover might see a deep crater ahead, and send that information back to Earth. The Earth-stationed human controller would signal the rover to change course and avoid the crater. But by the time the radio signals had completed the round trip, the rover might have fallen into the crater.

The rover needs to make such a decision on its own, without waiting for instructions from Earth. Yet, a Mars rover couldn't work entirely without human direction, because no one knows what might be found on the surface of Mars, or on any other planet. No planetary rover could be preprogrammed to handle every unexpected emergency.

Intelligent robot independence combined with human control

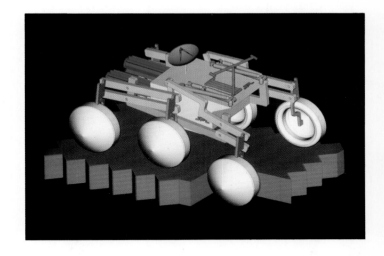

This computer design was the first step in making the Mars rover.

A simplified model of the rover has been built at Jet Propulsion Laboratory.

when it's needed is one solution to this problem. And scientists at Massachusetts Institute of Technology have come up with another possible solution.

At MIT's Artificial Intelligence Lab, prototypes—meaning working models—of planetary rovers have been developed that are small, lightweight, and made of inexpensive parts. The six-legged robot named Genghis weighs about two pounds and resembles an insect. Genghis can raise its legs and put them down one at a time to scramble, antlike, over rough terrain.

MIT's Rodney Brooks, Anita Flynn, and Colin Angle think rovers will be miniaturized even more. "By scaling down and using smaller motors, which could make do with tiny power supplies, we could gain a tremendous advantage," they say. "Most of the components we are interested in for our rovers—the computers and sensors—can fit on a small silicon chip. Why not put the entire robot on a chip?"

They envision thousands of these gnatlike rovers carried easily into space in a small payload. Spread over the surface of a planet, the fully autonomous robots-on-a-chip could explore much wider areas than a single large, teleoperated rover would. There'd be so many of them that if some failed to work, or fell off a cliff and broke, it wouldn't matter. And since they'd cost so little to make, they'd be left behind after reporting their findings to an orbiter. A cruel reward for loyal service? Since robots are machines, they couldn't feel abandoned, left behind on a planet in outer space.

Astronauts sometimes have to step outside their vehicles to

MIT's Colin Angle (above) adjusts Genghis, a full-scale prototype of a small planetary explorer.

A large rover (left) would require some teleoperation to help it avoid obstacles as it scoops up Martian soil samples to send back to Earth.

work in the dark empty realm of space. For human astronauts, this extra-vehicular activity (EVA) is scary and full of risk. Could robots replace humans in handling EVA tasks? Many people think they should, in order to reduce the danger for astronauts.

During a shuttle flight on the Atlantis in 1985, astronauts Jerry Ross and Sherwood Spring left the spacecraft to put together a metal frame, the kind of structure that will soon be used to build a space station. Later, at the Oak Ridge National Laboratory in Tennessee, a technician and a teleoperated robot working together assembled the same kind of structure the astronauts had built in space. An engineer directed the robot's movements from a control station, watching the procedure on television monitors. Although they took three times as long as the astronauts had, the team of technician, engineer, and robot successfully assembled the frame.

Certain scientists have begun to believe that some day, robots will be able to work *without any human input at all*, making every necessary decision to run themselves, by themselves. This is a fascinating possibility for all of us to consider.

Certain jobs require hands-on operation. Two astronauts in space outperform a technician and a teleoperated robot doing the same job.

Technician and teleoperated robot took three times as long to put together a frame as astronauts Ross and Spring had, but they got the job done.

No matter how human Manny
appears, he just can't think.
Researchers spent three years and
two-and-a-half million dollars
to create Manny.

Manny, the robot used by the army to test protective clothing, not only looks human; he can do many human things. He breathes: His chest expands and contracts, exhaling moist air. He sweats: Tiny tubes two to three inches apart on his skin surface emit water into the clothes he's wearing. His computer programs signal hydraulic cylinders to move pistons in and out, letting Manny bend his knees, rotate his shoulders, kick a ball, and salute a superior officer. His skin is flexible and warm to the touch.

Twelve researchers spent three years developing Manny. They used state-of-the-art technology in the fields of robotics, microprocessors, bioengineering, computer graphics, and materials science to design him. But in spite of his lifelike anatomy and computer-driven movements, Manny comes nowhere close to being human, because Manny can't think.

The human brain and the computer both have memories. A computer can store enormous amounts of information in its

Robot: *Tell us the secret of life.*

Man: *I tell you I cannot. I cannot create life.*

Robot: *Then show us what we must do. The Robots can do anything that human beings show them.*

From *R.U.R.*

memory, far more than a person can. In a memory contest between humans and computers, computers win.

But thinking is more than just remembering. It's recognizing numbers, letters, people's faces, and voices. It's learning things by seeing patterns emerge from the millions of bits of information people are bombarded with. For instance, when a baby hits a pot with a spoon, it hears a satisfying clang. The baby quickly learns that spoon hitting pot equals clang. Thinking is

The baby can identify a ball better than a whole roomful of computers can. And the baby lifts it more skillfully than a robot does.

also *reasoning*—creating brand-new concepts and ideas. Said Nobel scientist Albert Szent-Gyorgyi, "Research is to see what others have seen, and to think what no one else has thought."

Human evolution has given the baby, and you, five separate senses: sight, hearing, touch, smell, and taste. Robots already have all those senses, and a few extra ones too. They can hear higher and lower sound waves than you can and they can detect nuclear radiation, infrared and ultraviolet light, radar, and ultrasound. But just detecting sensory information isn't the same as understanding it. To understand, you must perceive, interpret, and reason. Your own magnificent brain lets you do all this.

All your senses work together to inform you where your body is. Not just whether you're in Ashtabula, Ohio, or on top of a mountain in Colorado—sensory feedback informs you whether your fingers are pointing at the sky or resting on your hip. Whether your feet are on sand or on rocks or in water. Whether you're breathing damp, moist air or campfire smoke. Whether you're hearing rock music, a coyote howling, or total silence.

If you touch a hot pan on the campfire, nerves in your fingertips send instant messages to your brain, and your hand pulls back faster than you can think about it. A robot has no nerves to tell it when it touches something hot or hard or soft or gooey. This ability is called tactile feedback. Researchers are trying to develop it for robots, but it's in the earliest stages of development. The simplest method to let a robot finger know it's made contact with a surface is by switching an electronic signal on or off. In another experimental method, little pads on the robot

In a Swiss candy factory, a robot using an artificial vision system sees where a piece of candy fits into a box.

fingers are filled with liquid. The movement of the liquid when the fingers contact something can be calculated to measure pressure. This primitive robotic sensory feedback can't begin to compare to the fast, accurate responsiveness of human touch.

Robots not only need to feel what they touch, they need to recognize what they see. Many robots have television cameras for eyes. TV images are broken down into tiny geometric patterns. The basic measuring elements in visual systems are called picture elements, or pixels. On your television screen pixels appear as tiny dots. One of the ways a robot can identify a nail or a bolt, for example, is by its shape, because every pixel that's part of the bolt outline is coded as a one, and every pixel outside the bolt outline is a zero. The code for the bolt shape is then stored in the robot's computer memory.

So far, artificial vision images have been very simple, like a caricature of a famous person you recognize even though it's drawn with just a few lines. But just imagine having to program a robot to recognize every single shape you see around you! Transistors and microcomputers have become tiny, but they're still not small or fast enough to match the size and power of human brain cells.

Cameras trained on a conveyor belt let a U.S. Postal Service robot see and sort mail. It searches its memory to identify shapes.

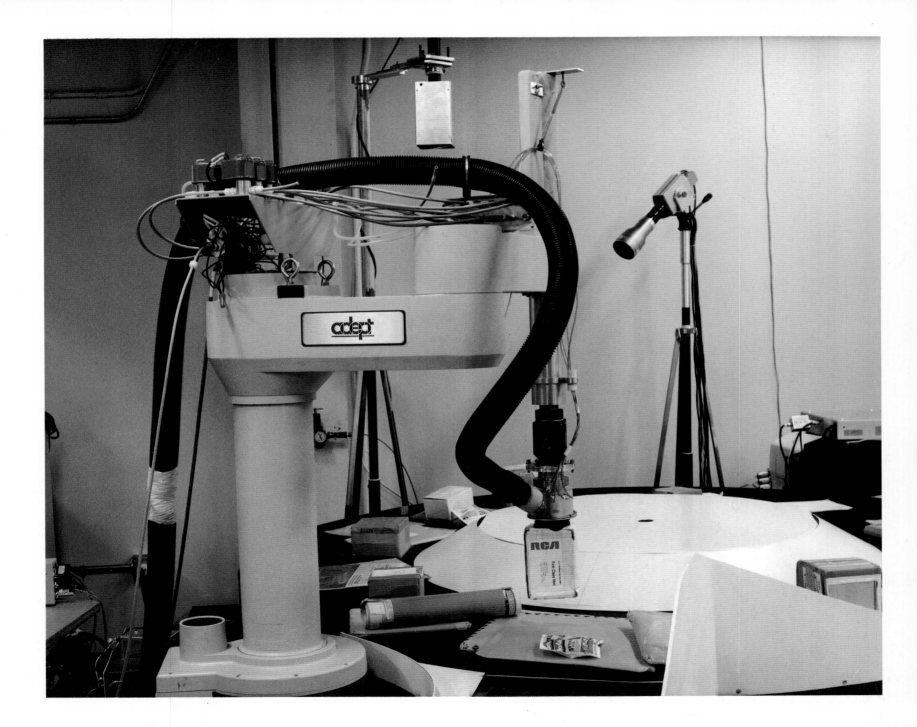

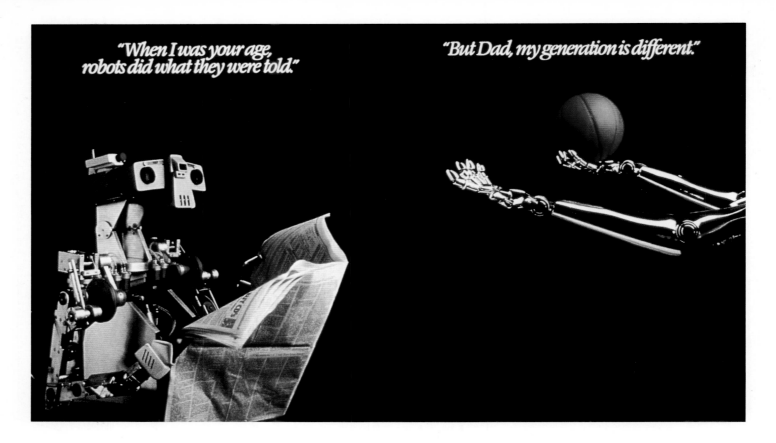

"When I was your age, robots did what they were told."

"But Dad, my generation is different."

Every year, robots are able to process more information. They've even learned to make intelligent choices by themselves. Some century, perhaps, they may become as intelligent as people.

The retina in your eye has a hundred million specialized cells and four layers of neurons that can do about a billion calculations per second. Sixty percent of your total brain is used to process visual information, in color. A hundred thousand supercomputers, wired together and all working at the same time, *might* match the visual capability of your brain. Or might not. No one knows for sure. Your own brain is vastly superior to even the most advanced robot brain in existence today.

If robotic vision and touch systems can ever become perfected, will robots then be as smart as people? Hans Moravec, director of the Mobile Robot Laboratory at Carnegie-Mellon University, thinks so. He says, "We are very near to the time when virtually no essential human function, physical or mental, will lack an artifical counterpart. The embodiment of this . . . will be the intelligent robot, a machine that can think and act as a human."

Fifty years ago J. M. Barnett, who built Elektro and Sparko, declared that no robot could ever take the place of a human. Today, Dr. Moravec predicts that fifty years from now, robots will be as smart as people, and that in a few centuries, they'll surpass humans in every way.

Not all scientists agree with Dr. Moravec about the future abilities of robots. Reality has a way of throwing roadblocks into the paths of dynamic new theories. But looking back to what robots were only thirty years ago, no one can fail to be impressed. They've come a long, long way. Every year they're able to process more and more information. They can already reach certain decisions by themselves. ALV, the Autonomous Land Vehicle, knows how to change its course to avoid an obstacle. Yet, humans had to program ALV to teach it to make a choice.

How far robots can eventually go is exciting to think about. But for now, you'll have to do all the imagining. Robots can't do that. Not yet.

# Some Milestones in the History of Robots

| | |
|---|---|
| 1515 | Leonardo da Vinci built a mechanical lion for King Francis I. It moved forward and opened its chest to show the lilies of France. |
| 1738 | Jacques de Vaucanson created a mechanical duck that ate, walked, and quacked. |
| 1774 | Jaquet-Droz, father and son, invented a clockwork doll that could write a letter using real ink. |
| 1801 | Joseph Marie Jaquard devised coded punch cards for weaving patterns in silk on looms. |
| 1890 | Thomas Edison developed a talking doll. |
| 1921 | The word *robot* was spoken on stage in London, England, in the play *R.U.R.*, written by Czechoslovakian author Karel Čapek. |
| 1927 | Westinghouse built its first mechanical man, named Televox. He responded to whistled signals from his master. |
| 1942 | Isaac Asimov originated the word *robotics* in a short story called "Runaround." |
| 1946 | ENIAC began operating at the University of Pennsylvania. |
| 1954 | George Devol patented a programmable robot arm; punch cards controlled its movements. |
| 1958 | IBM introduced computers made with transistors instead of tubes. Texas Instruments invented the integrated circuit. |
| 1962 | General Motors installed the first industrial robot in a factory. |
| 1970s | Silicon chips revolutionized computers and robots. |
| 1973 | Cincinnati Milacron marketed the first industrial robot controlled by a minicomputer. |
| 1976 | Robot arms were used on the Viking 1 and 2 space probes. |
| 1982–88 | Robots cleaned up radioactive contamination at Three Mile Island. |
| 1989 | Carnegie-Mellon University established the world's first four- and five-year Ph.D. programs in robotics. |
| 1990 | A robot arm on the Space Shuttle Columbia caught a bus-sized satellite and brought it on board. |
| 2001 | A rover, both teleoperated and autonomous, will land on Mars. |
| 2006 | The U.S. will face a shortage of 675,000 scientists and engineers.* |

*From a report by the National Science Foundation, 1989

# Index

# Acknowledgments

My warmest thanks go to Ed and our engineer daughters Jan and Lauren for their patient explanations; to Martin Ackerman of Hewlett Packard for twice reviewing and authenticating this text; to Stephanie Henkel of *Sensors* magazine for invaluable information and advice; and to Rita Hanover, who instigated the idea.

To all the scientists, engineers, and executives on the cutting edge of technology who granted interviews and shared their expertise with me, I offer profound appreciation: Gay Bogardus of Transitions Research Corporation; Roy Williams of the Center for Engineering Applications; Julie Carroll of the University of Utah Center for Engineering Design; Keith Henry of NASA Langley Research Center; Greg Koller of Battelle Pacific Northwest Laboratories; Charlie Ruch of Westinghouse Historical Collection; Scott St. John of MIT's Artificial Intelligence Lab; Ron Yukelson of Long Beach Memorial Medical Center; Wendy Keiper of Dinamation International Corporation; Larry Anderson of *Robotics World* magazine; Alan Hitchcox of *Hydraulics & Pneumatics* magazine; Sandra Dornan of ABB Robotics, Inc.; David Hall of AVG, Inc.; Peter Zentz of Benthos, Inc.; Tom LaPuzza of Naval Ocean Systems Center; Robert Kemelhor of the Johns Hopkins University Applied Physics Laboratory; Norman Baker of Baker & Nieman Enterprises; and Elliott Miller at Martin Marietta Corporation.

I thank all the people who generously provided materials and information at Texas Instruments; Jet Propulsion Laboratory; Adept Technology; Heath Company; the University of Western Australia; Utah Museum of Natural History; Festo Corporation; Lab-Volt; Denning Mobile Robotics, Inc.; Exos, Inc.; Carnegie-Mellon University; Prab Robots, Inc.; Cincinnati Milacron; USX Corporation; the U.S. Postal Service; and to Samuel French, Inc., for permission to quote from the play *R.U.R.*

Most of all, I'm deeply grateful to my editor, Barbara Lalicki, who believed in this book from the start.

## Photographs courtesy of:

AVG, Inc., Frontispiece; Battelle's Pacific Northwest Laboratories, pp. 6, 52; Westinghouse Historical Collection, pp. 8, 9; Dinamation International Corporation, p. 10; Utah Museum of Natural History/John Telford, p. 11 (left); Festo Corporation, p. 11 (right); Lab-Volt Systems, p. 12; ABB Robotics, Inc., pp. 13–15; Goodnight-Sweet Prints, p. 16; Texas Instruments, pp. 19, 20; USX Corporation, p. 21; Cincinnati Milacron Industrial Robot Division, pp. 22, 24; Prab Command, Inc., Kalamazoo, Michigan, p. 26; Center for Human Service Robotics, Carnegie-Mellon University, p. 28; Transitions Research Corporation, p. 29; International Robot Technologies, p. 30; the University of Western Australia, p. 31; Heath Company, p. 32; Denning Mobile Robotics, Inc., p. 33; Mike Milocek/University of Utah, p. 34; Waseda University, p. 35; Long Beach Memorial Medical Center, Long Beach, California, pp. 36, 38; Photography by Byron Wood, pp. 39, 40; Ed Rosenberger, Rosenberger Productions, p. 41 (left); © Exos 1989, p. 41 (right); Naval Ocean Systems Center, pp. 42, 43; Benthos, Inc., pp. 44, 45; Martin Marietta Corporation, pp. 46, 54, 58; the Jet Propulsion Laboratory, California Institute of Technology, Pasadena, California, pp. 47, 48; MIT Artificial Intelligence Laboratory, p. 49; NASA Photos, p. 51; Adept Technology, Inc., p. 56; U.S. Postal Service, p. 57.